The Gold Book
Volume 3

The Girl With The Notebook

I WILL BLESS THE LORD AT ALL
TIMES;
HIS PRAISE SHALL CONTINUALLY BE
IN MY MOUTH
PSALMS 34:1

Don't allow what's happening to you in the physical to distract you from what God is doing for you in the spiritual…. Catch it!
- @ officialayanayv

Them: what is your sign?

Me: the cross

Them: are you a Virgo?

Me: I am a child of God

- @ mhh_tinasia

I think it's kind of crazy that God is the only one who has a perfect track record, but he is the one we trust the least

@ therapyandprayer

Why would I be with a man who doesn't open doors for me physically, when God opens doors for me every single day

- @ conqueringasya_

God can't bless you with more
when you too busy settling for less…
catch it!
- @ officialayanayv

Shade from a tree that bears no fruit

should not bother you

- @ c.dovaaa

You speak on me

without you knowing me for real

makes you a fiction writer...

unpublished and critically acclaimed

- @jstnfrtt

Them: you think you're the prize?

Me: yeah,

and only a winner would want me…

clock it.

- @ camilleviviana_

The reason the devil is disturbing your peace

is cause your peace disturbs him…

catch it!

- @ officialayanayv

Tie your shoes and quit tripping

- @ baby_gurl1984

If I ordered a truck full of dumbasses

and I got just you...

I would have gotten my money's worth

- @ cammi0505

One time in an argument a man told me
he wanted to give me a piece of his mind
and I responded,
"well, I couldn't possibly take the last piece"
@ rebmasel

I don't care if you're a supervisor,

sun visor,

advisor,

or a Budweiser...

you're going to talk to me like

you got some sense.

- @ djcharliecharrr

You better scramble like an egg

before I fold you like an omelet

because I cannot people today

- @ rileygmitchell

If you are going to sleep on me,

do not wake up

- @ mynameisronnae

Look, I might be a handful,

but you have two hands

\- @ ky_mom_swag

I am the hot dog,

and you see I only have mustard on

because y'all cannot catch up to me

@ thickerthancoldcornbread

I don't think anybody has pissed me off

to the tip of piss off mountain

like you have sat here

and pissed me off

- @ ingyslove

See, this is why I said
you are intellectually anoxic
because you're saying things
as if your opinion matters.
- @ tallmetelly

The quicker you realize

that you're not everybody's cup of tea,

but............

you'll still be sipped

- @ inmariewestan

Them: you love me?

Me: im not going to prove it today

- @ san._ce

How are you wearing Dior

And

you are NOT wearing deodorant

- @ Jacob_amanyire

How mean would I be

if I tell somebody

that they only got a tablespoon

of ponytail?

- @ imkbfool

Men cannot believe woman are single

by choice

because men aren't single by choice

- @ lazy_gourmet

If I lost weight

the way I lost my mind,

I would look like a shoelace

- @ rileygmitchell

On my soul, I hit harder
than Chinese algebra
and faster than
Mexican music.
You will get whooped!
Stop playing with me.

- @ hersheyy.kisses_

This weather is so inconsistent…

just like these men

- @ jaylahiman_

Some people are out here

live, life, loving

but I am out here

crying, cussing, and struggling.

- @ thatstollerkid

It is way too much pressure

to be your everything

when I barely want

to be your little bit

- @ Jasmyn_carter

My crayons are sharp,

the box is full,

and bottle of glue is topped off

and my helmets on tight

- Gaheathen

Him: you have a bunch of hoe friends,

what does that make you?

Me: a gardener.

Keep a tool in the shed.

- @ ashastrother880
- imjusttooreal

If life is already beating your tail,
why are you bothering that lady
that'll do the same?

\- @ gigi_leflair

I'm not gone lie.

I do know my worth

but sometimes…

I be having a little sale.

- @ jc_nyc4

THANK YOU

TO EVERY SINGLE PERSON

WHO FOLLOWS ME ON SOCIAL MEDIA.

THE GOLD BOOK

HAS 3 VOLUMES

AND MORE TO COME:

GOD WILLING.

HEY GUYS!
PLEASE GO AND FOLLOW
EVERY PERSON MENTIONED
IN THIS BOOK.
THEIR SOCIAL MEDIA HANDLE
IS CITED UNDER EACH QUOTE.
SUPPORT! SUPPORT! SUPPORT!
I PERSONALLY
THANK EACH PERSON CITED!

IT SAYS IN JOHN 15:5 NKJV;

"I AM THE VINE;

YOU ARE THE BRANCHES.

HE WHO ABIDES IN ME

AND I IN HIM,

BEARS MUCH FRUIT;

FOR WITHOUT ME

YOU CAN DO NOTHING.

I LOVE JESUS.
JESUS IS THE WAY,
THE TRUTH
AND THE LIFE.
JOHN 14:6 NKJV

GOD IS SO AMAZING!

Made in the USA
Columbia, SC
16 February 2025